# DOCKSIDE
## EXTRAS

**STAGE 2**
**BOOK 1**

# NOT A SMART PLAN

Philippa Bateman

# RISING★STARS

JJ sat on the step to eat his hotdog. "Oops!" he said as a trail of red goo slid down his T-shirt.

2

No. The green one with the GB flag.

Quick as a flash,
the T-shirt was off.

**1.** What did JJ have in his hand?

**2.** What sort of flag was on the T-shirt?

**3.** What was JJ's plan?

*Find the words to fill the gaps.*

**1.** JJ, have you seen my _____ T-shirt?   (page 4)

**2.** I need a _____ plan.   (page 8)

**3.** Mum might _____ it for me.   (page 10)

*What's missing?*

**1.** jj sat on the step to eat his hotdog   (page 2)

**2.** no the green one with the gb flag   (page 5)

**3.** ooh that is not a fresh smell   (page 12)

*Put the **verbs** (drop, looking, crept) in the right gaps.*

**1.** JJ _____ away.   (page 10)

**2.** I'll _____ it in the bin.   (page 10)

**3.** _____ for this?   (page 12)

*Put it right.*

**1.** I smart a need plan.   (page 8)

**2.** this for Looking?   (page 12)

**3.** that is not Ooh, a smell fresh.   (page 12)

*Swap the word in **bold** for a new word that means the opposite.*

**4.** I need a **smart** plan.

**5.** JJ **crept** away.